ALCHEMY OF
HALF-DEAD GODS

JADEN EYZENBERG

Contents

Preface

Alchemy of Half Dead Gods was, in a sense, not truly planned. Poetry was simply the way in which I was able to make sense of the suffering I had undergone in my life—put a leash on it, polish its fur, even teach it a few tricks to make it presentable. Eventually, though, what started as a therapeutic exercise metamorphosed into my first full book *and* a true passion project (obsessive late night revisions and all). I had attempted to write other books before, sure, but they all seemed facsimiles of what literature should be. By this, I mean that however well crafted my sentences, however well chosen my words, I could not rid myself of the sense that I was writing a lie. This is not to say that writing something that is good and something that is true is mutually exclusive (god knows this book isn't exactly perfect), but as I sit here typing out this little blurb I know that the words to come are justified. They are the narrative I had been searching for in every other work I had previously undertaken. They are a cohesive, yet (perforce) utterly disjointed explanation of some of the most harrowing moments in my life. They are the emotional outpouring of memories stamped onto paper the very moment of their recollection. They are mine, they are raw, and they were very painful to translate to the printed page.

Before you get an opaque view into some of my worst days, a brief clarification is warranted regarding the format and content of this book:

- The thread that stitches this whole book together is disillusionment and recovery from trauma. Although the poems are separated into implied clumps by person and/or occasion, they are organized to convey the (overarching) healing process in all its grizzly ardour.
- Names of specific individuals have been kept hidden for obvious reasons (hopefully that's enough to not get me sued), but there should be enough context clues for readers to put the pieces together.
- If some portions of a poem seem utterly incomprehensible, it was most likely deliberate. There are references within that no one but myself and the people these poems speak of will have any likelihood of understanding; which is exactly as it should be. Some things I'd just rather not explicitly write out.

Thanks to Covid-19, I detest overactivity on social media and screens in general; on the off chance that I do amass a following, however, my instagram is @jeyzenberg.

With all that out of the way, dig in.

Prologue

Let not your heart be withered to a stone
The tender sun will even fry a flower
with rays; the same by which the petal's grown

Not when your lover's laughter turns to groans
And thinks your yearning hand a grab for power
Let not your heart be withered to a stone

Nor when your gilded father is dethroned
Weeping at the table while you cower
And shrinks in size since you can only grow

Nor when your mother reaps what she has sown
The son unshackled by his eighteenth hour
Let not your heart be withered to a stone

Not even as the cuffs dig into bone
Since mother cannot lock you in her tower
The court will hold your key, as now you're grown

And least of all when *they* yearn to atone
But you're no longer one who sings in showers
(My heart, by then, was withered to a stone
with rays—the same by which the petal's grown)

Impressions from a night I don't want to remember

1.

The candles smolder low

Incense poisons the air like mustard gas

She lies in her linen sick-bed

Pale, as the pill bottles on her nightstand

Are her wine glasses,

And she swirls them as such when

No one is looking

2.

Spiders live inside her throat

They spin gossamer gowns

out of guilt

For her silver tongue

(Always a perfect fit)

A shadow glides across the wall,

and the smoke falls into step behind it.

Both are by her side now,

but the fumes have robbed her sight

It is her ex husband's face

she discerns through the smog

3.

Ointment glistens in a

hand that can't be mine

Rub it on me

Cobwebs expel from lips

Attach to it like puppet strings

Her voice pulls the threads taut

And the hand, like a marionette, obeys

While the shadow watches

helpless

I envy it

4.

No, not like that

Lower, lower, lower!

Somethings not right

She can reach that herself

Why is her breathing so ragged

why? why? why?

I? I? I?

Not me, not that, not mine

5.

As cream lathered keratin

crosses the rubicon

A pair of eyes-

they can't be mine-

Shift away

There is a man on the balcony

Staring from the other side of the window

I do not recognize him

I do not see where his hand went

His face is on fire

6.

Swiftly it is done

Her jaws swing shut

and the wires go flaccid

The floor is surging up to catch

my plummeting

for a lifetime

Body

My?

Freud's I is looking down on it

From the stratosphere

With the blanching seraphim

It is so stupidly limp

Even as it burns

Soldier Boy Without a War

A soldier hunkered down in my pocket—
the only thing they let me keep in the cell.

My grey-green talisman, 1940's tough, seemed to
oxidize where it lay;

(strange, since there was hardly anything to breathe
down there).

While the air, stagnant as swamp water, grew damp
from our cold, collective sweat.

Yes, we were fried by those humming, hanging
facsimiles of sun,

but that is not why we sweat
—all of us, except my copper figurine.

My great grandfather carried it into war because we
wanted to massacre ourselves a second time,

but valiantly;

Once, it had steered his pilot-sense against the
wehrmacht,

but there it was sitting in my damn pocket with its
hands in its own pockets and its rusting head down
as if to say 'we are both resigned to this nonevent.'

No explosions, no shrapnel, no gunfire to tantalize the "how long until?" Just interminable valleys between the hours and the understanding that killing time in a cell is far less grandiose than killing Germans out of one.

In retrospect, however, an analogy:

> delay is to criminal justice as fallout is
> to atom bombs.

(It's waiting in the ruins of aftermath that kills you from the inside)

The Unwilling Oedipus

I do not wish to crawl again
Inside my memory, deep
Alas my torments never end
When setting off to sleep

The loafing mind is set to work
In place of idle hands
Remembrance does more than lurk
When free of life's demands

As such, I stand outside her door
A varnished, ghastly white
While knowing soon I'll serve again
Jocasta's dark delights

Where You End and I Begin

My heart did not beat without your say;
For it was hard to tell it was mine at all
As you reached through the atom gaps in my ribs
With fingers slender as serpent tongues
And made blood dance at your leisure.

Neither did my lungs draw breath without your urge
—so is it fair to say *I* was the one breathing?
Your anger strangled the oxygen from life,
choked me like a noose till you
cut me down, a pardoned criminal.

Neither did my eyes shut for blissful sleep;
not when you were howling into the night
and the wolves answered back.
What audacity it would have been to dream
when nightmare stalked among the waking!

Speaking of,
did the night ever blot the sky
without your permission?
Or was darkness merely tissue paper you
pinned to the ether with thumbtacks
we mortals call stars.

Did the sun ever sparkle in defiance?
Or was it merely your glare that loomed
so high
and big
and bright with the light of god

it threatened to blind us?

I built altars to appease you,
Led the congregation in prayer too:
"Forgive me mother for I have sinned"
I used to lay it on thick for you
that much is certain

I thought every sinew
Every ligament, every tendon,
That held me together was you.
And that if your nostrils flared I
would come apart in a cluster bomb
of limbs dissolve into shape and
dissipate into the wind

I know better now,
Just so you know.
I matter, I am matter
That thing that has mass
And takes up space,
Has its own place.

Know too, that if I could
I would saw myself in half
Cell by cell
Just to purge myself
Of any trace of you.
That even if it left me half formed
And half man and half dead
It would be worth it to have
No part of, in, or from you

But you will not know
Not until you have made
congress with the earth
and worms have learned
your name

And I will stand six feet above
You, towering as I once remembered you
And cry with no shame;
not for your demise
But for how even death cannot
take you
Far enough from me

Post Traumatic Anger

This coat of apathy is one
outburst too small.
Its hairs are prickly.
They scratch like a razor burn.
I cannot wear it,
I should not wear it
while this incandescence of mine
This white hot, mounting discontent melts
the carpet we're playing monopoly on.
And if my teeth don't stop grating like tectonic plates
the ground will shake and splinter into all the missing
pieces that would've made me whole
(had it just broken earlier).
But catastrophe is superfluous now,
Huddled in a molehill
along with the afterthought of an apocalypse;
dwarfed to insignificance
by my own last name.

None of that really helps
when the air
crackles plasma-like
At my passing,
simmering,
and the dandelions
I try so hard to wring the joy
out of crack
and wither at my touch.

My head feels like a pressure cooker. What is this

Squirming tangle of nerves
frayed by the years doing
between my temples?
Some writhing spaghetti tangle
you can tug on at any time to unravel me.
But if you did, it would all just liquify
and coalesce into fluid rage until sopping before you
Is the amalgamation of every hidden part
I never wanted you to see.

Of course it's hard not to see.
Hard not to notice blood drip from the soles
of feet that have to balance
on a razor wire of control.
Hard not to notice how I flinch
When an engine gallops past with doppler fury,
or whenever the blender flays the air
with that noise, noise, *noise* of distant wailing,
screeching pierce-the-peace-of-velvet-night-scream.

Or maybe those are just my own metal
folds grating against each other.
You think I glow with
life? Ha!
Don't be fooled by friction sparks.
I am a gasping
thing

No more alive than those wind up toys
children crank with their grubby fingers.
Children whose laughter minces my eardrums;

(with that noise, noise, *noise* of distant wailing,)

grinds them until I dream of taking their grape-heads
And beating them into wall-pulp.

It's just an imaginary
grape-stain-fresco of a someone else, but I look down
and see it's
eight year old me that's the someone else.
He who didn't get to cry or else they'd give
him something to cry about;
that someone else.
How should I explain to those mushy else's
I did it for their own good?
Any louder and
the ghosts that hide in the attic of my mind
would've come
downstairs and...and...

And being made of rubber is exhausting.
I'm always pulled taut at both ends,
and when I'm stretched too far I
never know the end result. Will I snap
back and be rendered idle elastic?
Tear, perhaps, and fling the grips on either half
to the wayside? Probably, I'll just flutter
to the floor--stretched too thin to do much else-
and kiss the linoleum;
Not passionately, but exhausted of my own passion.

Passion is exhausting, you know
Feeling like you're trapped in your own exoskeleton,

Being boiled alive by all the things you
bite down on your tongue
to prevent from oozing out
is exhausting.
Feeling like you radiate threat-
watching **them** scan the space between your brows
 for a trefoil stamp that says:
"ionizing, keep away!"-
 is exhausting.

I'd like to say being radioactive has its charm.
At least they know to keep their distance, but maybe
I underestimated how hollow the room becomes
when you expel everyone that you wish
would hold you instead of running the other way.

I don't want to be angry anymore.

Dentist Appointments Make It Bearable

I lacked the nerve to swill tequila dreams
Nor pump my veins with mist to send me dreaming
Novocaine cocktails, I had once felt
Were blameless brews to guide me to un-feeling
My cavities were prophecies revealed
My joy, however, never quite revealing
I relished my mouth's numbness with a stealth
The pliers would not pry along with teeth that they were
stealing

My heart which raced for lack of any thrill
Found peacefulness a pace not quite so thrilling
So used to trauma's all pervasive chill
It found the absence of it all too chilling
Thus when they stabbed my gums with evil drills
That heart would leap for joy at all the drilling
Since the pulse with which my chest and head were
filled
Went silent as they hammered in the filling

I could not tell you why I felt relief
Beyond the nerves the dentists were relieving
Perhaps I lulled myself into deceit,
That anesthesia spread its calm deceiving
To regions other than the gums that bled
(Though grateful was I ever for the bleeding!)
And grateful I was too for dental health
Though mental was the thing that needed healing

Prayer vs Pubescence

Me and G-d used to
play peek-a-boo.
He hid in black leather boxes
And the spaces between yud-hay-vav-hay
(But only if read right to left).

Then came the big thirteen
And I didn't like what I read
between the lines

The people of the book taught me
to hold fast to discipline with
a white knuckle grip, the way
you'd hold a siddur's spine; yet

When I stumbled into teendom
(you cannot waltz into acne and erection)
I learned that bodies were a bit more than
meat sacks for the soul to rot in. Cannibal
appetite drove me, I plunged
into flesh sans grace—God's or otherwise—
surfacing

Only to repent, to take half breaths
as my half hearted sorries were
gasped out, or read out…cried
out, maybe, before diving again

Sins of the anatomy are atoned for
by anatomy:

40 lashes on each arm
to appease the festering sages
And my budding manhood

It was the sweetest agony I had ever known
The release made sweeter by the return
From filth to faith
Transgression, a routine
Repentance, a formality
Our private ritual of deceit neither of us believed
But both wanted to
At least I had the decency to hate myself for it.
That has to count for something right?

How could I abstain?
Desire beckoned like sunwashed dewdrops are
beckoned by the breeze to leap beyond petal edge and
detonate into the earth with reckless abandon;
—To hell with the fall, it's the sudden stop

.

.

.

.

.

.

.

That kills you!

Rituals

Close the door
Once
Twice
And recite ten synonyms for remorse
Only eight? Fine, but it's coming out of your sanity

Keep your head covered, bent of course
Know who it is you're standing before
The almighty Genesis 38:8-10 demands

                                        What?

Knowing is for heretics

                                keep quiet shoulder devil

Only one was supposed to be here
But you're perched beside both fears

Now repeat after me: *Baruch Atah*
No, not like that! Your tongue is twitching again
Do it

                                                Over

                                Over

            Over

Overboard?

Sounds like sin when you say it slow

Oh alright, take the damn pills!
But angle the pillow to cover your crown
So the finger of god doesn't prod it while you sleep

Little jew head poked through like paper mache
Shema yisrael seig heil to your nazi god

Desert deity occupying a parched soul,
want some tea?

> How
>   does
> a
>   yid
> make
>   tea?

He-brews it in the boiling stew his brain's made into
by thinking of every reason not to flip a switch!

Funny, isn't it?

Defy me, will you?
Can you withstand the synapse attack
Of not choking enough on the "ch" in challah

Or perhaps you'd renounce Him altogether;
sprint for the faithlessness you're already wading in.

Defy me, will you?
Please

Abnegation

1.

Here lies the sacrosanct,
buried with the Amalakites
The Midianites
The Canaanites
The torturous nights
of fake supplication.
Euthyphro has fallen.
Job is vindicated.
But at what cost?

Better honest and godless
Than a two-faced saint.
Still, now whirling in this
maelstrom of possibility
I might just choke on air.
A thousand winds compel me
A thousand gusts to carry me
'Round the world back to where
I began: certainty.

2.

Killing your idols is far from glamorous.
I tossed my prayer books into a trash bin
And instead of lightning forks,
idle chirping and ill-suited sunbeams
Mocked the anticlimax. The world
did not tilt off its axis.
The stars did not plummet into the sea
to hiss and steam and die.

The words of the prophets just-
(how else can you say it)
just plunked onto the wrappers
like a sigh amidst life.
And if the flies had ever heard of holiness,
they certainly didn't show it.

We Both Knew How It Would End

*"Those whom God would destroy he would first
make blind"*
-something you once said

If the sun were to be extinguished right now
By the sweat of a universe fearing its own
annihilation
We would not know for at least nine minutes

Merciful water-logged molecule of ours,
hurtling through the blindness

—for our benefit?
                            doubtful

Did you think gravity,
something,
locked us in place?
No, it's all relative motion:

Attraction of big things to bigger things to bigger
things
To the biggest thing in our allotted divot of space-
time
Beguiling us with constancy

It's a web of celestial wedding rings
Our earth just one bride in this planetary promise
Trying to keep pace with itself
As it careens through the ultraviolet froth—
With us as fortunate voyeurs

I chime in:
Are the things we want to last white lies?
The crease in the crook of a newborn's lips?
The eyelids still struggling to unfurl?
Subject that to a star's death, would you-
Would God?

(The truth is, I'm scared of being happy around you
while the dopamine dies with the retreating daylight

—How do I know this is just a sunset, and not the
prolonged end of something bright and beautiful

But the way your skin sticks to mine
whispers immortal,
so I'll hazard the question)

The answer lurked behind the reflection of your
glasses
(third new pair this month)
Surely yearned for me to ask
And just like that, we're right at the beginning

Missing You

Sometimes I write little love letters with the dust
That collects on my window.
Specks of dead skin and dead hair
Part in my finger's wake
Like sea before the ship
To make room for the lack of you.
But every time I hope to see your face
Between the motes
The only thing in the gaps
Is my own reflection staring back

Self Pity

I was the line break between you and
happiness in your yellow journal pages,
bird forever straining for flight

Formerly the anchor pulling at your heel
and hurling you back down to earth.

Tugged away from your beloved height,
You coughed and cursed the dust and me alike
For having the nerve to want to settle

I was the wretch worth keeping out

The eyes that want
The hands that need

(*how diminishing, to be the one that needs*)

I used to wish I was anything to you
Other than a grasping greed
But one thing most of all:

I longed to be an ant
So that on the day I pretended not to stare

As you defied your 63

for a cup to cradle your tea

I could leave a trail of ant kisses

on the fingernails I crawled between

And you wouldn't blame me for it
Since I'd be such a meager thing

Don't worry, I've stopped wishing

Mothman

Hail to the mothman
Singing his gospel to any unfortunate

That mistakes him for newspapers
Piled on a park bench.

He's a panther stretching awake with audacity,
Whiskers too gray and long-lived to bother being proper

He's a man whining with gusto
Voice almost as hoary as his fur.

If your curiosity gets the better of you,
(And it will)
You'll agree to glimpse at what's in his pocket-

A polaroid browning at the edges-
Its him, he'll say, him and his never-love

Standing side by side.
He's holding her hand

Just well enough to hide a wedding ring
That he didn't give;
That wasn't his to give.

It stops short
like a good man's life
Where two (smiling?) faces should be.

"I tore the top off," he'll say to you,
And then mutter something about treachery.

"Couldn't stand to look at her."
His throat tightens
The spider veins bulge like in the photo.

He wishes he hadn't, he'll say—

He can't remember her face

Hail to the mothman
letting the unfortunate go

Just in time for a battalion of limping dark
To violate the day.

Just in time for the moths to huddle 'round the lamps
Who've bowed their heads in shame
of the gleam that drew their visitors.

The moths batter the glass
Yearning for the what's beyond it

Every night dashing themselves against steel and
circumstance
While he looks on.

Once and only once

I saw him take a rock
And make like Goliath against cruel fate

He shattered the glass to shards
And one by one he watched them flutter in,

Watched their paper wings flash,
And dance in bliss and die and die and die.

Mercy, he called it

Dear Memory, (unfinished song)

You never asked for my love
But I've never prayed to be scorned
So you're right that the page we were both never on
Is better off now that it's torn

Dear Memory

Ship of Theseus

Let's say, for a second, I was anything
other than hurt.

What of grandiosity?

Of dark looks in high places?

What a fantasy!

A grief to be so dense if you balance it on a rainbow
it turns to glass   and snaps in half

Oh, humor me, will you?!
Tell me that suffering isn't just a curtsy—
theatrics

that ghosts stop stirring the wind and laughing
leaves cease their pageantry
if the right wronged person passes by

Tell me an orange is more wound than peel
even though I just skinned one alive

Say I'm not
mashing myself to pulp just so people
have something to whet their pallet

                    [My tongue for the chance
        that these words unstick themselves from the page
                    and thumb-knuckle your spine]

God and Wisdom Aside, We're Still Going to Die

The lump that crawled into grandma's throat
Had butterfly wings
And a moth's appetite
For once
Not the bastard child of my sarcasm
But I repented of it nonetheless,
all of it,
and spoke
softer than I ever had
To this wilting titan
Who hoisted our too-large home
For us lonely few
On her creaking shoulders every day
Had her hair always been so gray?

In my room, the walls
were devoid
Reminding me we're all just
marionettes
Hurtling towards death at the speed of fear…
Or maybe that was all in my head

It's probably nothing
Denial lurked under the covers
Where I hid
Or rather,
It was the plastic plant on my desk
The stuffed lion fraying at the seams
And my bedside stack of dead men's ink
That mocked me for even trying to

And to all those philosophers I devoured,
Those who crammed oblivion
Into their twelve point font:
Some wisdom that was.
Casting a candle into a canyon doesn't make it any
brighter
after all
But some want to see the wrinkles in their rock
If only seized briefly by
grasping flame and mind
Although seeing some etched in the face of mine
Made me long for the thankless dark
But I knew then

This was our lot.
God tried to clean us up
But we
splashed the soap into his eyes
So he left us
to the dirt and dust we were made from
And would become anew

Although,
there was one redeeming irony:
Blinded as he was, I knew he wasn't watching
So I knelt
and prayed to a tumor
knelt and prayed to a tumor
Which at least had a chance of being benevolent
Or was it benign…

Smokers

Even the earth's cathartic mounds are allowed a drag,
So why not me?
Moreover, how many times have I thought to myself
Damn I could use a cigarette
When I don't even smoke.

Maybe because the birther
almost burned alive while
Surrounded by faucets and drains
All that water going nowhere
and still, flame
Later, wrapping the fear in rolling paper
To be close enough to what all but killed her
Souvenir but mitigated,
embers for the inferno of self,
Teeth for bone, calcium microcosm
Maybe she's hoping cigarettes can finish the job
At least, I did

Or her father,
Filtering fumes since seventeen and subjecting us to
Car seats which reeked
of carcinogens through and through
Despite his cell sickness—which didn't even need
motion;
But always smiling,
decay of a grin glinting yellow like his
headlights. A childhood chauffeur.
I barely noticed the aroma when I hugged him
Post schism, though

It wasn't the scent that made my eyes water
And when my father asks, I say the fallout has been
dulled by time,
not memory

Maybe her brother
Drifting like smoke on whatever winds billow his jacket
Today, Bronx
Tomorrow, Brooklyn
With kids whose fingers got too big to catch or chase
vapor
A real wordsworth's kind of cloud
True, having a sister brand you as smog
doesn't encourage you to stay the weekend
But sometimes they did share the warmth
of a lighter passed between them—
Ceasefire for the daily dose of death

At last, me
Lounging on a moon warmed bench
Now, end of the chain of being
Later, who knows?
There's so much dew huddling on the grass
my hand seems to cry with just one brush
How fitting that the air only vaunts its moisture
in the silent,
sightless dark
How like us!
Maybe I'm more atmosphere than volcano after all. I
mean,
Contaminate versus fumigate?
Clearing the air really depends

on whether you breathe
Pyroclasts or not
(these sequestered words)
but what the hell!

Everyone that's ever loved and sighed has drawn breath
and died
Oxygen will do
Might as well curl three fingers
pinky up
Then raise to lips,
kiss the emptiness before parting ways
Breathe in, breathe out
And pretend its smoke that's flying away

Papa's Weekend World

Cars sedated by traffic
Amble down the highway
Like a caravan of souls.
Their reluctant headlights
Flash SOS in the black rain

From inside your honda
The world looks vague.
I savor this: the way a snowglobe
must be when the shaking stops
And the glitter simply falls

The wetness drumming soft
its fingers on the windows
muffles the incoming calls

You're speaking heroism into
existence—dungeons, goblins,
How my deft swordsmanship
turns underwear to scraps. I laugh,
and it cleaves the sky like thunder

But the glass is still intact

Daddy Killed the Wasps

age twelve—I leaned on the wrong corner of a country fence
gone, a backwood haze born of dry bluegrass
gone, tiny thumping feet, laughter

true, I was the first victim of my blunder,
but its carcass reserved a grave
for the coming holocaust.

sting-pits (battle scars, you said) bloomed
purple and ugly on my palm
there was no time for a hospital.
you used honey and tweezers to extract the barbs.

then in bed, as I convalesced
You donned a god's anger
and extracted penance from
the gnashing of mandibles

perhaps You stole upon the nest
just as the wasps were tucking
their larvae into bed. Perhaps

they saw nothing
but an inscrutable pall
and the almighty spray can before they died
—understanding nothing

justice is blind,
but fathers stare undaunted at their gruesome work;
so by the time justice blinked the blindness

from its eyes—too late! You let billow
the killing gas. now the wasps poke
out their hapless heads—too late!
now their corpse clumps seep yellow-black
from their buzzing, paper swathed globe:
the collateral of innocence, the ichor of an alien wound.

You came back inside aglow with death, as though
rebuking my indiscriminate pity, poured
brutal truth of wasp blood and epiphany
in the scripture of my burning hand as I slept:

If it was enough to be a good man, You'd have let them live

But men cannot be good without being good

at what men must do,

can they

Rhymes for a Snowbird

Decembers made breathable by your south-bound flight
I descended from my bedroom in a teenage crouch
To paw at the upholstery of our corner couch;
lime shade fading—like my adornments to your might
Our phone calls were fonder once you'd alight
Unsaid by same-sounding voices on both ends
And unseen too by stubbled faces so alike could pretend
Absence makes the heart grow fonder:

Is that right?
Fonder rendered possible by yonder was our plight
Not that your proximity repelled this absentee,
But I sensed the way a wind-battered apple
was being blamed for falling
from an already distant tree
The root of the problem, as I see: a calendar
Enforced on you, obeyed by me
By a mother of two, and the bane of three

Water under the bridge, hopefully
Whose beams must maintain their interval
Lest the thing that spans crumbles again
into that departed sea

Father, grateful am I for the roof you provided me
Yet had I known we'd be its fluted columns
Crushed under supporting the cover, damned to liminality
I'd have risked the rubble shower
And ushered in dark ages by toppling a decadent Rome
If the havoc meant that sooner I'd been able to come home

When the rain subsides

I've walked the copse with soporific steps
When the leaves were not and when leaves were there
I've seen the evergreens—their promise kept
But found I'd like the whorled branches bare
I've lived such pleasant dreams on benches old
I've loved the grass that grows without a care
And woke to life again in burning cold

I've watched the plastic mare the schoolboy rides
He used his phantom reins to gallop bold
Until the rushing rain could not abide
A man but one who with the storming wept
And when the flowers were at last denied
The gravel road and I were both bereft
As not a single lovely thing was left

Ex Nihilo Nihil Fit

Exult in the lacerations above (but not) me
Pink as a pleasant dream, light spilling
From an otherwise aging bundle of sky. What if I

too could bleed luminous
in my evening hour?

Is that something reserved for the vast
we can only grasp—no—grope at
from our own dusty corners.

We are the ones who shade
our face with finger nets

        upon confronting the ideal after all...

But not I,

        I am no hypocrite.

I will weep with the willow's namesake even
In the bower reserved for lovers;
Contaminate with my tears
The stuff of sonnets just to feel something

So when the clouds cut themselves on the edge
Of twilight   (how petty, time is)   and the fleshy
wounds
Of smoke echoes trickle down,

down

    my

        outstretched

                arms

                        their blood shall run

so as not to profane the offering
Of things born so soon and dying sooner

Yes, world, I am your joyless god but
Gaia's gore plucks the sympathy from my rusted
heartstrings

Even on a day like this

I knew I was free when

I took a detour on the way back to my dorm
just to drink the twinkling trees
and twinkle with them too.
They reminded me of freedom's first glimmer:
The screaming red and blue and red and blue
siren song of mustaches and badges
and hullabaloo
It was freedom like using expired peace
To fertilize fresh disaster
And being the one to plant the seed
With my own hands

I was free when I drove down
to the station to have them bound
Without even washing off the dirt

Later, in the back of the van
I sang along with Johnny Law
who said he'd never seen a happier man in handcuffs

(I was free to take it as a compliment, so I did)

Even when they told me not to smile for the mugshot
I was free to tuck a grin in the corner of my mouth.
And once they took me
Down down down
I slipped it out and giggled at it;
What else to do when you're buried alive in a tomb
And the headstone reads: here lies the old you—so
chicken shit

It had to come to this

I am in my room
I am on my bed
I am far away from that tomb
I am free to close my eyes and browse
The shaded hall of my pupil's memory
It's free to remember the humorous things:
The god-awful cheese sandwiches that disintegrated
before you could even take a bite;
Or the Russian with the tiger tattoo,
Roaring rip-tooth safari on his grass-swarmed arm;
or the black man with biceps so big
they'd break through our cell before his sleeves
And it's a wonder how they squeezed into either

But regardless, our wrists were all shackle-size
So the tiger was leashed
The wild biceps tamed
And now I know why my eyes glistened when I saw
those trees

Because when they strung us together like christmas
lights
It was nothing like spreading my arms so wide
I could hug those trees thrice over
and still have arm to crucify

That day, I was made to march to a gavel's tune
But now the trees sing my wrists
will never touch again
And I never want them to

First Draft: **Judgement Day**

They strung us together like
Christmas lights
Alibis not as iron clad
 as our wrists
We do not twinkle
Where the light don't shine
But we made a conga line
And marched to a gavels metronome.
It sounded like this:
Da-dum
Da-dum
What fun!
You're done;
Send the next one in

Children Play God When They Play in the Snow

1. SNOWFALL

I trudged to the heart of the campus green

And all around me, lamps bled blue and stood vigil

—A crown of fat black thorns.

As the blizzard swam through their clouded light,

It seemed the sky was grating off

The fluttering shards of its bones—

Fell like a crumbling snakeskin in the night.

Come morning, a thousand little hands

Will mold life from the remnants

Of slow fallen skeletons.

2. REMINISCENCE

A man that is not a man

That is a boy

Matches boots to the imprints he left behind

In the snow.

After hours spent in the cold, his lips

Match the shade of the little pills he takes

To keep whole.

In the raw, white silence, a man

That is not a man

Can hear the chattering teeth of a boy

Curled under his blankets.

At the sound of breaking glass

He shivers, waiting for the sirens.

When does he get to be warm?

3. THE RIVER HERACLITUS MISSED

On the other side of the Susquehanna

A dirty snowman stands, patiently waiting

For the first flicker of the rising sun.

From where I am, the iced carrot nose,

The pebble smile and three perfect circles,

All seem to mock me with their wholeness.

I cross over to meet its challenge

But now, so close,

It stops smiling

I realize that it had never smiled.

Crossing again, I leave behind dark waters

Still held immutable by the season's sidelong glance

While knowing the river won't change

—Not in this weather.

4. SUNRISE

From behind a thin membrane of clouds

The sun forces out its lukewarm light

In sputters—first breaths taken

by the almost-drowned.

Soon, the Chickadees that live by the river

Will have their way with the snowman's eyes.

Then, lacking, they will stake their futures

 on what life was preserved by the snow

Tended by the warmth of a blanket

I had bought for myself, I resolve

That after the birds have had their fill,

Before the children check their creation,

I'll take a look at what's inside that snowman.

Maybe, if I'm feeling whimsical,

I'll even help them put it back together.

The Sea is Death

I can picture it now
The bloated sea in the end times
Has reached the limit of its forbearance
It can devour not one more gaze of a crepuscular
dreamer
For it has dreams of its own
Not another saccharine rhapsody of a sunset bard
In its salted catacombs
Heaving,
Roiling,
Coral crusted black molasses
A wet, maddening surge will herald its revenge
Nevermore shall the sea require
to carve out a home
As earth's very latticework stretches wider in welcome
One last frothing baptism,
And all sentimental blasphemy washed away
by the moon-tossed tide.
Standing atop their last refuge,
Those bards, those dreamers
Shall tremble in revelation:
The sea is not the tranquil surface
it permits the terns to knife with impetuous wings
The sea is not song-stuff limerence
To be stashed in pentameter
and decanted at one's leisure
Like vials of wine-dark poesy
The sea is death
A bubbling alchemy of half-dead gods
swirls unfathomable in its yawn

The sea is a patient, ravenous beast
Licking cliffs down to bone
Slurping sand with its foam
Eon after nameless eon.
And come the last one,
'Enough with erosion,' says the sea,
'It is beneath my splendor,
Now heed:
In the beginning there was darkness
And darkness there shall be
For in the beginning there was darkness
And the darkness was me.'

She forgot to feed you, younger brother

I knock on the door
Of the four-walled afterthought
She stuffed you in

And wade into
computer heat,
electric whine,
dust, dust, dust

Your insomnia eyes
don't leave the screen

I leave you mac n' cheese,
orange and crusted and semi hard

Sorry, I could not
make the noodles supple
I used water instead of milk
and microwaved it in a bowl

I leave you disappointment—
Your rightful inheritance

your face a jumble of age
(plump baby cheeks, translucent
mustache, dead brown tooth)

reads: thanks for the new socks
Fuck

> but an hour later

The bowl
outside the door is filthy
But the spoon,

that damn spoon,
licked clean

Birth and Circumstance

In the car, his exhale spans fathoms of road
while the day strips its vermillion gauze,

a mawkish little whore
"I never loved her, you know"

* * *

Sweat, shame, the distant regret
of a potent summer

left its taste on my father's lips
after the primordial deed;

The most humane violence
is biology

* * *

Rings cracked teeth on their own metal tails
Fingers green bleeding

White wedding dress faces:
The bride and the groom
I do, I do, I do

* * *

Bones in the lacquered bowl
sizzled with prophecy

Polaris shuddered like a wet cat
as causality mimed its conjury: "come forth,
come forth, child of sin and weakness."

I do, I do, I do

* * *

An empty closet haunted by
a conversation never had.

       The suitcase bulged, fat and nauseous…

Her bed is cold.

* * *

Silence crouches on gargoyle haunches
and bares its fangs

even as I fiddle the radio knob—as though
the right response was hiding in a frequency

The image of her standing there that day
comes to mind—runny nosed madonna,
mouth agape,
A still life of professed, perfect victimhood

"I never loved her either."
"You don't really mean that."

I think I do, I think I do, I think I do

"...fearing the chronic angers of that house"

Often, I have to handle rats because my field of study demands I know how to compel a thing more trivial than even an undergraduate like me.

Some students resent it when they dig their claws into you as you pick them up, but I figure it's less a defensive response and more their desperate clutching onto the only familiar chaos between cages.

* * *

Bathed in the scent of hand sanitizer
and the red haze of laboratory lights,
I watch one dart at the dispenser's click
and recall that me and my brothers
knew to scurry to our rooms by the sound of her
footsteps,
and that snoring
meant tonight we might just sleep.

How does my little, fumbling, furry fuck
feel about all this?
Dignity aside,
I'd like to think that being the plaything of giants is
tolerable
considering that even B.F. Skinner
—pasha of pigeons, raja of rodents—
still had to end all of his experiments
by cleaning vermin shit.

Speaking of cleaning shit, in 1975 they did an
experiment
where rats were administered inescapable shocks
and the global forum of spectacles
got their "mhmm's" in when it was found
that futility precedes the human condition
—by which I mean eventually every one of them
    laid down and took it.

now I'm not saying people are exactly like rats,
 but I remember being told yet again to toss mommy's
"pills" and "herbs" into the trash bag
 before the sirens got any closer
 and I grumbled the whole way through
 but my stepfather, loving husband, dumped
 capsule after capsule after capsule
 stiffer than an arcade claw machine

while his frozen lips flashed: *don't be a rat.*

Every action has an equal and opposite reaction

so maybe apathy on a cosmic scale

is a bit exaggerated.

Hard to imagine an indifferent, threadbare universe
being the same one with the Third Law of Motion
stitched into its hem:

shove a wall and the wall shoves back.
Punch it for not moving aside,

now your purple, puffy knuckles have been formally
acquainted with reciprocity.

That throbbing logic—good ammunition
as I wage war with 11 A.M.:
release me from my covers!

Why battle the earth's metal neck yank
If there's no omnipotent right hand
At the other end of the chain?

Well, yes,

but better to whine on one's feet
than gripe on one's back—(thanks Zapata).

So I rise,

gravity shoving down my spine, and incessant Newton
cupping my heels.

 I stand,

compressed by the fundamental forces of the universe,
every platitude under the stars.

I walk,

forcing another step through the eye
of an ever resisting cosmos
because that's the only way to make it say it cares.

The carpet bristles against my soles
as it's done for nineteen years,
And all I can do is be grateful.

Ship of Theseus II

"I came not to send peace, but a sword"
-Matthew 10:34

I, levite on the altar of manhood:
Here we go again,

Anointing my chin in jeopardy twice a week
to slice the complacence from my cheeks

A fitting thing,
maturity and razorblades—
to be the same

Foam folds into the contours
of my neck, worn pathways

on the trek
to a clean face, a clean stubble slate
taunts miles and miles
of scabs away

This is shaving:
like grief, a balancing act

Too hard and it leaves a scar
Too weak and you won't be sleek—and whatever the
bible says about the meek

Inherit the earth?
Try applying the aftershave

and not wincing
before dreaming of conquest

You want the planet as your own
without stepping on any toes?

He who is without sin
rubs stones flat
while working up the nerve
to throw them

Although,

My courage was come to
by clock hands fleeing one another
—ironic

Too long for me to realize you take a blade to lip
And come out better for it

speak sharp to a parent,
a friend, a love
and come out respected for it

Wolves get empires, and sheep
get gloves
(A shame they named me after a dove)

Both won't be touched
but for entirely different fears

So be the thing with whiskers and devil ears

One clean pass, then two,
three cuts on the jaw, I'm through

The worst of it, the hair
floats in the sink like pollution

I tour the marks with a finger
hoping one day they'll be scars

And what do you call tracing scars? Poetry

Notes and Acknowledgements

This project could not be what it is today without the tireless efforts of my illustrator, Akbar Hasan. His assiduity, promptness, and communicativeness went leaps and bounds into making the commission process as smooth as can be.

Likewise, credit is due to my editor: the perceptive Shelby Newsom. Although she may not have realized it (sorry Shelby), her remarks on the vagueness of certain parts of my poems were an indication that I had struck a good balance between disclosure and secrecy; After all, I can't tell every sordid detail of the little I've revealed about my life.

Finally, allow me to commend my typesetter and cover artist, Euan Monaghan. As someone who has only just gotten into professional authorship, Euan went above and beyond in explaining the minutiae of interior design to me without my even requesting it; Initiative for the uninitiated is few and far in between these days.

* * *

The title "The Unwilling Oedipus" derives from Sophocles' *Oedipus Rex*.

Both "Ship of Theseus" and "Ship of Theseus II" originate in a metaphysical thought experiment posed by many ancient philosophers, but formalized by Plutarch in ⬚*heseus*.

"Ex Nihilo Nihil Fit" is a latin saying that translates into "from nothing, nothing comes". This dictum was first postulated by Parmenides, as discussed in Aristotle's *Physics*.

"The River Heraclitus Missed" references the age-old adage of Heraclitus which states: "No man steps into the same river twice, for it is not the same river and he is not the same man."

"...fearing the chronic angers of that house" is a line taken from Robert Hayden's "Those Winter Sundays".

"Every action has an equal and opposite reaction" is taken from Newton's Third Law of Motion.

About the Author

Jaden Eyzenberg is a 20 year old amateur poet born and raised in New York City. While he currently lives in Brooklyn, Jaden spends most of his time in Binghamton where he attends university as an undergraduate psychology major. Assuming writing doesn't yield immense riches, Jaden intends on going into a counseling and/or educational role for obvious reasons.